THIS
JOURNAL 😍
BELONGS TO:

―――〰〰〰〰〰〰〰〰―――

MY EMOJIS

© London & Ardre Orie 2017
All Rights Reserved

All rights reserved. No part of this publication may be reproduced, distributed, or transmitted in any form or by any means, including photocopying, recording, or other electronic or mechanical methods, without the prior written permission of the publisher, except in the case of brief quotations embodied in critical reviews and certain other noncommercial uses permitted by copyright law. For permission requests, write to the publisher, addressed "Attention: Permissions Coordinator," at the address below.

13th & Joan
500 N. Michigan Avenue, Suite #500
Chicago, IL 60611

www.13thandjoan.com

Praises for My Emojis

We need to teach girls vital skills to develop the character necessary for good decision making in the pursuit of their happiness.

> — Dr. Rose-May Frazier
> Director of Advising First,
> Florida State University

There is only one you. My Emojis helps every girl embrace her uniqueness.

> — Eboni Dotson, Wife, Mother,
> Healthcare Professional

My emojis is just what my daughter and I both need to remember our worth in a fun and expressive way!
— Dr. Keita Joy Ductant, EdD, M.S.
Motivational Speaker|Success Coach
www.keitajoy.com

There is only one you. My Emojis helps every girl embrace her uniqueness.
— Dazi Lenoir, Maddie's Mom,
Attorney,
Owner at Legal Lyons Law Firm

My Emojis

LONDON & ARDRE ORIE

This book is dedicated to our family for loving us eternally.

LO & AO

Girls have the power to rule the world!

Table of Contents

I. Dear Girls 1
II. Introduction 3
III. My Emojis Journal 5
IV. Who Am I? 14
V. The Girl Power Game Plan 95
VI. An Open Letter to ME 105
VII. GIRLS RULE THE WORLD Challenge 137
About the Authors 138

My Emojis

I: Dear Girls

Dear Girls,
Hey you! Yes, of course you! Can I tell you something? I think that you are awesome! I've created a new book and you are reading it. This book was created to inspire you. It's a journal so, it allows you to write exactly how you are feeling. If you had an amazing day, you can write about it. If you feel like you've have a bad day, you can write about that too. You're growing up everyday and that creates a lot of new feelings. We should never be afraid of growing up. I know that it can be nerve wrecking, but it's natural. I get it, trust me. Not only do we have to make friends, but we also have

to try to learn about ourselves. There is so much that we can do, when we learn to be happy and have fun. Remember that the most important person that you will ever meet, will always be you. It's pretty exciting to know that you alone have the power to discover happiness. I hope that you enjoy this book. I wrote it with my heart just for you.

Love,

London Orie
#TheOrieGirls

 ## II: Introduction

No one ever said that it was easy to be a girl, but in the end, it's' always worth it! We began writing this journal together because we recognized the importance of feeling good about who we are inside. Girls can do anything when they know their power. We believe that #GIRLPOWER is a real thing! When we know how powerful we are, we can change the world and make it a better place.

Recognizing our power begins with understanding who we are and what motivates us. Our internal motivations are called FEELINGS. We call feelings EMOJIS, because EMOJIS help us to discover what we are thinking, even when we can't find the words. The truth is that we all have feelings, they makeup who we are. Our greatest potential is in recognizing those feelings and deciding what to do with them in healthy ways.

My Emojis gives girls valuable opportunities to learn about who they are and valuable strategies to deal with everyday feelings in a healthy way. This is essential to discovering #GIRLPOWER. You deserve to know that you are unique and special and that not one other person in the world is like you. It is our hope that you will remember that the most important person that you will ever get to know is YOU!

Love,
Ardre Orie
#TheOrieGirls

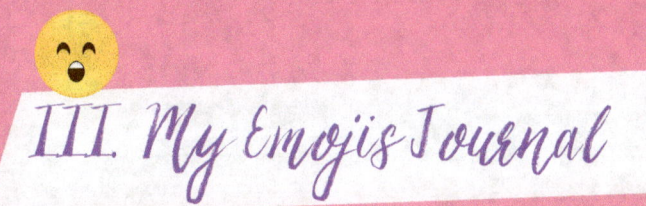
III. My Emojis Journal

We are most powerful when we know how we react to many different situations. Knowing exactly who we are, helps us to be the best version of ourselves.

#THEORIEGIRLS CHALLENGE

Try to answer one question a day to learn more about the amazing person that you are!

Thankful

That moment when you receive a present or someone does something really nice for you, thankfulness fills your heart.

Tell about a time that you were thankful.

Excited

That moment when you see your family after a long day at school.

Tell about a time that you felt excited.

Scared/Nervous

That moment when you feel embarrassed.

Tell about a time that you were uncertain of what would happen next.

Relax

That moment when
you get to unwind.

Tell about a time when you were allowed to chill.

Angry

That moment when you feel displeased.

Tell about a time that you felt upset with another person.

Silly

That moment when
you can just be yourself.

Tell about a time that you were happy just being you.

Love

That moment when you feel warmth in your heart.

Tell about something that makes you smile on the inside.

Confused

That moment nothing makes sense.

Tell about a time when things just didn't seem to add up.

Fearful

That moment when something bad happens in our world.

Tell about a time that something made you feel unsafe.

Tired

That moment when
you are in need of rest.

Tell about a time when you felt weary.

Pouting

That moment when you learn that things don't always go your way.

Tell about a time when you felt discouraged.

Disappointed

That time when things didn't
go as planned.

Tell about a time that you felt that someone let you down.

Crying

That moment when
you shed real tears.

Tell about a time that you were moved to tears.

Sick

That moment when
your body tells you to take a rest.

Tell about a time when you did not feel well.

Hangry

That moment when your hunger gets the best of you.

Tell about a time when your hunger made you unhappy.

Apologetic

That moment when you realize that you must right a wrong.

Tell about a time that you hurt someone.

Angelic

That moment when you do something nice for someone else.

Tell about a time when you put others first.

Fierce

That moment when you realize that you are amazing.

Tell about a time when you felt like the bomb.com.

Surprised

That moment when you had no clue about what would happen next.

Tell about a time that you were surprised in a good way.

Smart

That moment when you know how to solve a problem.

Tell about a time that you figured out a solution to save the day.

Queenin

That moment when you realize just how special you are.

Tell about a time when you recognized your worth.

Now that you've taken time to explore a variety of scenarios, it's time to dig deeper to discover who you are and how you are wired. Let's do this!

We have the power to decide who we want to be and the power to become it.

#THEORIEGIRLS

IV. WHO AM I?

Knowing who you are is essential. You can't be your best if you don't know yourself first.

#THEORIEGIRLS CHALLENGE

In the circle below, create an emoji that best describes who you are. Be sure to color it in.

THE BEST OF ME

You have amazing qualities that make you special. No one should be able to point out these characteristics better than you.

#THEORIEGIRLS CHALLENGE

Use the space below to answer each question and discover the best parts of you!

One of my best qualities is...

~~~~~~~~~~~~~~~~~~~~~~~~

~~~~~~~~~~~~~~~~~~~~~~~~

~~~~~~~~~~~~~~~~~~~~~~~~

One way that I show that I am courageous is...

~~~~~~~~~~~~~~~~~~~~~~~~

~~~~~~~~~~~~~~~~~~~~~~~~

~~~~~~~~~~~~~~~~~~~~~~~~

One way that I am creative is...

~~~~~~~~~~~~~~~~~~~~~~~~~~~~~~

~~~~~~~~~~~~~~~~~~~~~~~~~~~~~~

~~~~~~~~~~~~~~~~~~~~~~~~~~~~~~

One of the ways that
I show loyalty is...

~~~~~~~~~~~~~~~~~~~~~~~~~~~~~~

~~~~~~~~~~~~~~~~~~~~~~~~~~~~~~

~~~~~~~~~~~~~~~~~~~~~~~~~~~~~~

One way that I show kindness is…

~~~~~~~~~~~~~~~~~~~~~~~~~~~~~~~~~~~

~~~~~~~~~~~~~~~~~~~~~~~~~~~~~~~~~~~

~~~~~~~~~~~~~~~~~~~~~~~~~~~~~~~~~~~

One way that I fight injustice is…

~~~~~~~~~~~~~~~~~~~~~~~~~~~~~~~~~~~

~~~~~~~~~~~~~~~~~~~~~~~~~~~~~~~~~~~

~~~~~~~~~~~~~~~~~~~~~~~~~~~~~~~~~~~

My Loved Ones

A huge part of who you are, includes those who love and support you most.

#THEORIEGIRLS CHALLENGE

Add the names of those who love you in the heart below.

The Me I Want To Be

Far too often, the world tells us that we are bossy. Who ever said that knowing what we want is a bad thing? It's not. The challenge is learning how to communicate our needs and desires in ways that are respectful and considerate to those around us. Instead of being called "bossy", we are going to examine the word assertive. To be assertive is to express our desires and what we wish to have happen in a positive way.

Mirror Mirror on the Wall

The way that you see yourself is important. It never matters what others think. It's all about you.

#THEORIEGIRLS CHALLENGE

Use the lines below to answer the questions with words that best describe you.

Write 3 adjectives that best describe how you see yourself.

_____

_____

_____

Write 3 adjectives that best describe how you feel about yourself.

~~~~~~~~~~~~~~~~~~~~~~~~~~~~~

~~~~~~~~~~~~~~~~~~~~~~~~~~~~~

~~~~~~~~~~~~~~~~~~~~~~~~~~~~~

Name 3 of your best qualities.

~~~~~~~~~~~~~~~~~~~~~~~~~~~~~

~~~~~~~~~~~~~~~~~~~~~~~~~~~~~

~~~~~~~~~~~~~~~~~~~~~~~~~~~~~

Bossy or nah?

The truth is that we have all had moments that we were too assertive or not assertive enough. Not being assertive enough means that we are a <u>pushover</u>. Being too assertive means that we are <u>commanding</u>. Let's go deeper!

#THEORIEGIRLS CHALLENGE

Think of a time when you were a **pushover.**

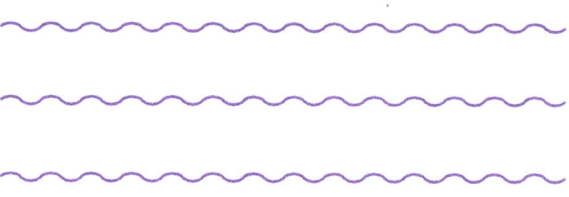

Describe what happened.

Describe what you did.

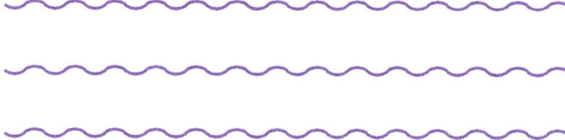

Describe how you felt.

~~~~~~~~~~~~~~~~~~~~~~~~~~~~~~~~

~~~~~~~~~~~~~~~~~~~~~~~~~~~~~~~~

~~~~~~~~~~~~~~~~~~~~~~~~~~~~~~~~

~~~~~~~~~~~~~~~~~~~~~~~~~~~~~~~~

~~~~~~~~~~~~~~~~~~~~~~~~~~~~~~~~

Describe how you believe the other person or people felt.

~~~~~~~~~~~~~~~~~~~~~~~~~~~~~~~~

~~~~~~~~~~~~~~~~~~~~~~~~~~~~~~~~

~~~~~~~~~~~~~~~~~~~~~~~~~~~~~~~~

~~~~~~~~~~~~~~~~~~~~~~~~~~~~~~~~

When we don't handle things the best way that we know how, we can always handle it better. That's real #GIRLPOWER!

-London Orie-

#THEORIEGIRLS CHALLENGE

Use the space below to list 3 ways that you could have handled the situation better.

1.

2.

3.

#THEORIEGIRLS CHALLENGE

Think of a time when you were **commanding.**

Describe what happened.

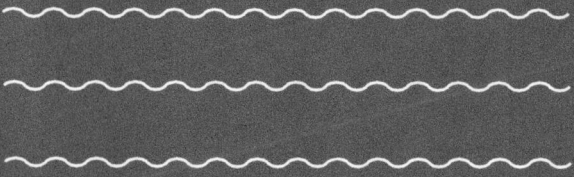

Describe what you did.

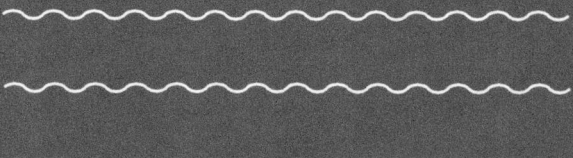

Describe how you felt.

~~~~~~~~~~~~~~~~~~~~~~~~~~~~
~~~~~~~~~~~~~~~~~~~~~~~~~~~~
~~~~~~~~~~~~~~~~~~~~~~~~~~~~

Describe how you believe the other person or people felt.

~~~~~~~~~~~~~~~~~~~~~~~~~~~~
~~~~~~~~~~~~~~~~~~~~~~~~~~~~
~~~~~~~~~~~~~~~~~~~~~~~~~~~~

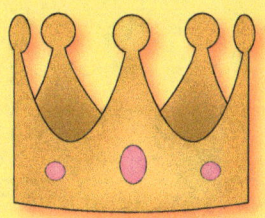

Being our best also means committing to learning how we can improve who we are and how well we treat others.

-Ardre Orie-

#THEORIEGIRLS CHALLENGE

Use the space below to list 3 ways that you could have handled the situation better.

1.

2.

3.

LOVING
THE REFLECTION IN THE
MIRROR

It is true that beauty is in the eye of the beholder. Never forget, the beholder is **YOU!**

#THEORIEGIRLS

#THEORIEGIRLS CHALLENGE

Take the quiz below by reading each statement and placing a checkmark in the box that most fits how you feel. You've got this!

	Strongly Agree	Somewhat Agree	Highly Disagree
I am worthy.			
I have something to offer the world.			
I am happy with the way I look.			
I have good qualities.			
I can do things that I set my mind towards doing.			
I believe in myself.			
I can overcome failure.			

Scoring:

Examine how many checks you have in each category.

If you have more checks in Strongly Agree, YOU GO GIRL! This means that you have a great sense of self and you can accomplish anything that you set your mind to.

COMPLIMENT HER

A true representation of GIRL POWER is when we can compliment others. It shows that we are secure in who we are and that we have the ability to recognize the good in others.

#THEORIEGIRLS CHALLENGE

Use each circle below to draw an emoji that represents a compliment to another person.

LOL

It is often said that laughter is the best medicine. Laughter can help us when we are not feeling our best and it can help to cheer up others when they are unhappy.

#THEORIEGIRLS CHALLENGE

Make a list of ways that you can bring laughter to brighten up the day.

~~~~~~~~~~~~~~~~~~~~~~~~~~~~
~~~~~~~~~~~~~~~~~~~~~~~~~~~~
~~~~~~~~~~~~~~~~~~~~~~~~~~~~
~~~~~~~~~~~~~~~~~~~~~~~~~~~~
~~~~~~~~~~~~~~~~~~~~~~~~~~~~
~~~~~~~~~~~~~~~~~~~~~~~~~~~~
~~~~~~~~~~~~~~~~~~~~~~~~~~~~
~~~~~~~~~~~~~~~~~~~~~~~~~~~~
~~~~~~~~~~~~~~~~~~~~~~~~~~~~
~~~~~~~~~~~~~~~~~~~~~~~~~~~~
~~~~~~~~~~~~~~~~~~~~~~~~~~~~

DON'T STRESS ME OUT

We all have triggers for getting stressed out. The most important thing that you can do, is learn about what can happen to create anxiety and stress. This information will help you remain calm.

#THEORIEGIRLS CHALLENGE

Place a checkmark next to the scenarios that get under your skin.

__ Arriving Late

__ Being Assigned A Ton of Homework

__ Appointments at the Doctor

__ Chores at Home

__ Being Asked to Make a Public Speech

__ Not Having Enough Money

__ Arriving Late

__ Meeting New People

__ Losing Something of Value

__ Appointments at the Dentist

__ Immunizations

__ Being Interrupted When Speaking
__ When Parents Don't Get Along
__ When People Are Unkind
__ When A Friend is Dishonest
__ A Test at School

#WWYD (What Would You Do)?

Sometimes we get angry when things don't go our way. We can be certain that everything won't go as planned. We must know the best ways to deal with life when they don't. Remember, challenges can make us even more powerful, if we make good choices.

#THEORIEGIRLS CHALLENGE

Use the space below to tell about how you would handle each scenario presented. Remember to be honest. You can learn a lot about yourself through your reactions to various situations.

Here's the Scenario	What Would You Do?
You told your friends that you would have a sleepover before asking for permission and then you mother tells you that the answer is no.	
You try out to sing a song for the school chorus but your friend is selected.	
Your teacher informs you that you will be having a math test on a topic that you still need help learning.	

Your friend tells you that she wants to sit with someone else at lunch for the day.	
You arrive at school and forget your class project.	
You decide to read a book and you learn something that you never knew.	
You overhear one classmate mistreated another classmate.	
You learn that your parents will be going out of town for the weekend and that you will be staying with your grandparents.	
You overhear two girls at school speaking negatively about you.	
You win the award for good citizenship at your school.	

Use the space below to write what you believe that your answers say about you?

~~~~~~
~~~~~~
~~~~~~
~~~~~~
~~~~~~
~~~~~~
~~~~~~
~~~~~~
~~~~~~
~~~~~~

RELAX, RELATE, RELEASE

Every girl needs to know what it takes to recharge. Taking time to relax and care for yourself must be a priority.

#THEORIEGIRLS CHALLENGE

Draw your dream sanctuary in the box below.

#THEORIEGIRLS
Name Game

It's important to know the traits and characteristics that you feel most represent you. Play #TheOrieGirls Challenge

Step 1: Write the letters of your first name vertically in the first heart below.

Step 2: Write the letters of your last name vertically in the second heart below.

Step 3: Using the letters of your name, create positive words that express your positive attributes.

Example:

L-LOVING

O-OPTIMISTIC

N-NEAT

D-DETERMINED

O-OUTGOING

N-NICE

O-OBEDIENT

R-RADIANT

I-INDEPENDENT

E-ECONOMICAL

FRIENDSHIP FAIR AND SQUARE

The qualities that you pick in your friends, says a great deal about who you are.

#THEORIEGIRLS CHALLENGE

Use each square below to write the qualities that you want in a friend, using the list of words provided.

POSITIVE FRIENDSHIP TRAITS

Understanding Giving Kind Honest Smart
Athletic Funny Helpful Courteous Trustworthy
Loyal Good Listener Dependable Expressive
Honest Supportive Confident

R.E.S.P.E.C.T.

Knowing how to communicate positively when situations arise in friendships is key.

#THEORIEGIRLS CHALLENGE

Imagine that you feel disrespected by a friend. What would you do? How would you communicate? Use the space below to create a text convo to sort things out.

V. The Girl Power Game Plan

It is essential to have a plan of action. Even if you don't follow every step, you must have a plan for who you want to be and what you want to accomplish. A girl with a plan is powerful!

#THEORIEGIRLS CHALLENGE

Use the lines provided below to map out a plan for your amazing life!

List 3 ways that you want to be more powerful...

List 3 goals that you want to accomplish...

List 3 people that you want to help...

~~~~~~~~~~~~~~~~~~~~~~~~~~

~~~~~~~~~~~~~~~~~~~~~~~~~~

~~~~~~~~~~~~~~~~~~~~~~~~~~

List 3 ways that you will make a difference in your community...

~~~~~~~~~~~~~~~~~~~~~~~~~~

~~~~~~~~~~~~~~~~~~~~~~~~~~

~~~~~~~~~~~~~~~~~~~~~~~~~~

List 3 ways to be happy...

~~~~~~~~~~~~~~~~~~~~~~~~~~

~~~~~~~~~~~~~~~~~~~~~~~~~~

~~~~~~~~~~~~~~~~~~~~~~~~~~

List 3 ways that you will help your environment...

~~~~~~~~~~~~~~~~~~~~~~~~~~

~~~~~~~~~~~~~~~~~~~~~~~~~~

~~~~~~~~~~~~~~~~~~~~~~~~~~

List 3 problems that you will solve...

~~~~~~~~~~~~~~~~~~~~~~~~~~

~~~~~~~~~~~~~~~~~~~~~~~~~~

~~~~~~~~~~~~~~~~~~~~~~~~~~

VI. An Open Letter to ME

7 REASONS TO WRITE A LETTER TO YOURSELF

1. To show gratitude to yourself.

2. To remember what made you smile.

3. To empower yourself.

4. To create a plan for the future.

5. To embrace who you are.

6. To remind yourself that you are amazing.

7. To share advice that you have learned along the way.

#THEORIEGIRLS TIPS ON WRITING A LETTER TO YOURSELF

It is awesome that you have decided to take the time to write a letter to yourself. You will be so happy that you did!

1. Stand in front of the mirror and stare at yourself for a bit.

2. Imagine yourself in this very place, one year later.

3. Consider what would you say to the girl staring back at you in the mirror.

4. Think about the most important things that you have learned over the past year.

5. Think about something that you did to help someone else.

6. Thank yourself for something.

7. Thank someone else for being a part of your life.

8. Consider what you plan to accomplish and who you want to be.

9. Write your letter with love.

10. Sign your letter from yourself.

11. Practice loving the reflection that you see in the mirror.

#THEORIEGIRLS CHALLENGE

Use the space below to write your letter. Keep it close to your heart and don't forget to come back and read it from time to time. You'd be surprised when you see just how AMAZING that you are!

VII. GIRLS RULE THE WORLD Challenge

Now that you've written down the best things about yourself, and learned about what motivates you to be who you are, it's time to take ACTION! Let's keep the positive thoughts flowing. We challenge you to 30 days of repeating words that remind you of just how awesome that you are. When you speak positive words to yourself, they are called affirmations. Let's work!

Affirmations.

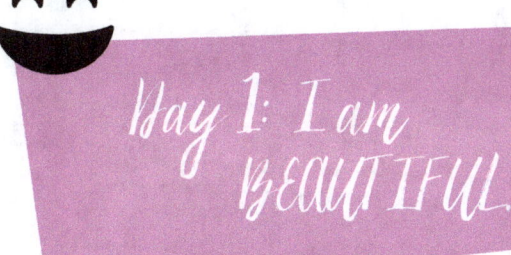

Day 1: I am BEAUTIFUL.

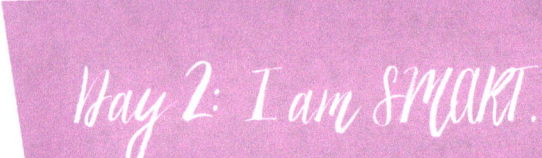

Day 2: I am SMART.

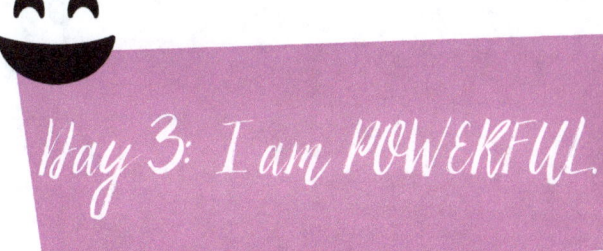

Day 3: I am POWERFUL.

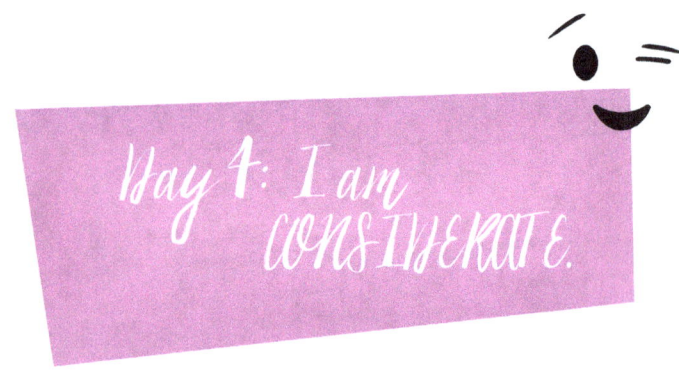

Day 4: I am CONSIDERATE.

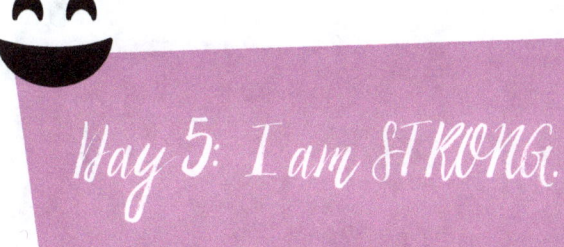

Day 5: I am STRONG.

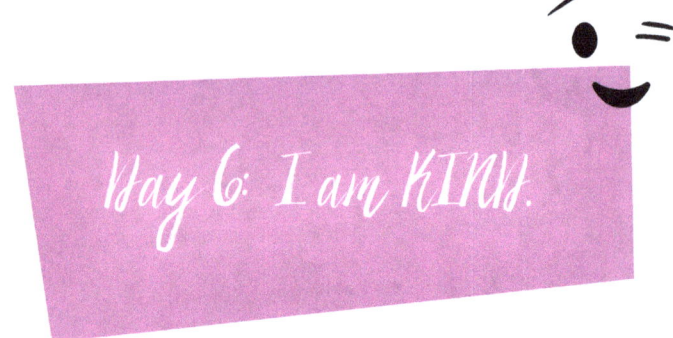

Day 6: I am KIND.

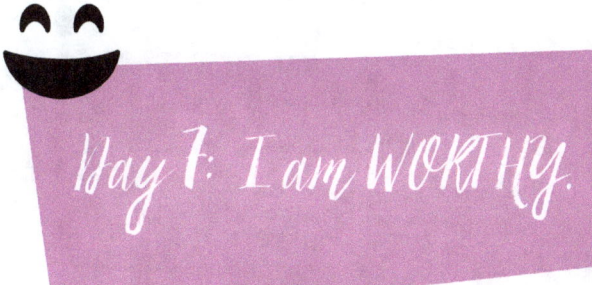

Day 7: I am WORTHY.

Day 8: I am CREATIVE.

Day 9: I am SOCIAL.

Day 10: I am a LEADER.

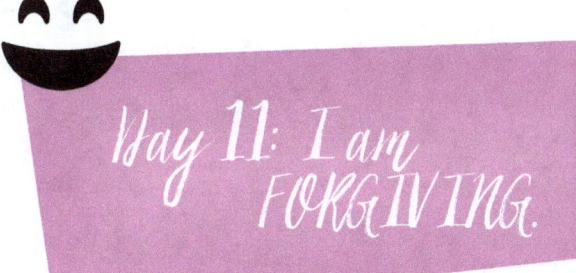

Day 11: I am FORGIVING.

Day 12: I am LOYAL.

Day 13: I am SUPPORTIVE.

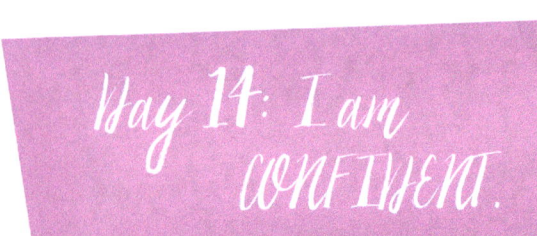

Day 14: I am CONFIDENT.

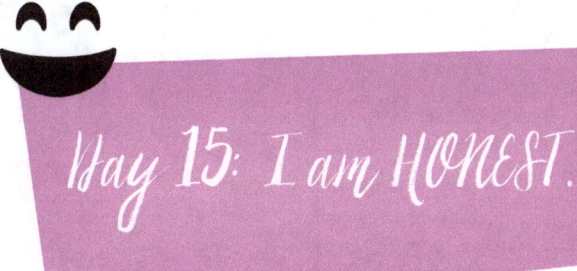

Day 15: I am HONEST.

Day 16: I am AFFECTIONATE.

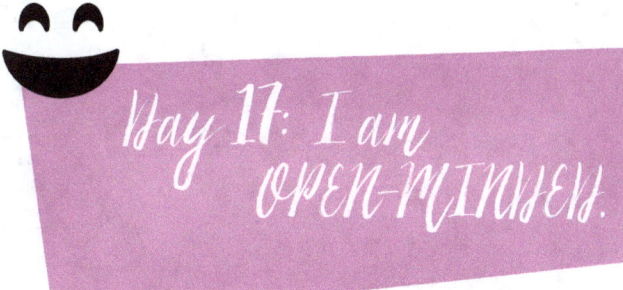

Day 17: I am OPEN-MINDED.

Day 18: I am PATIENT.

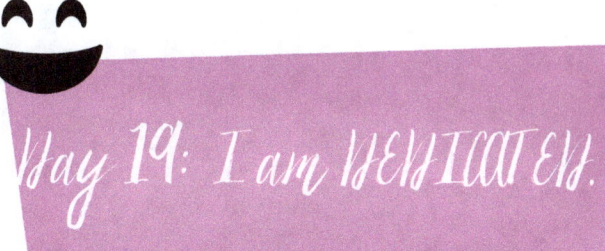

Day 19: I am DEDICATED.

Day 20: I am CURIOUS.

Day 21: I am FAITHFUL

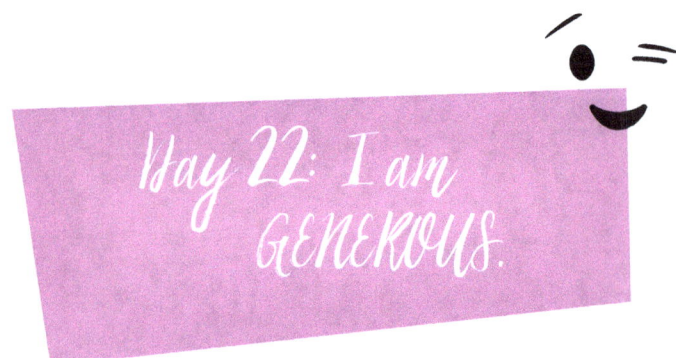

Day 22: I am GENEROUS.

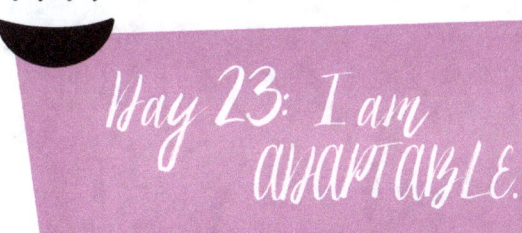

Day 23: I am ADAPTABLE.

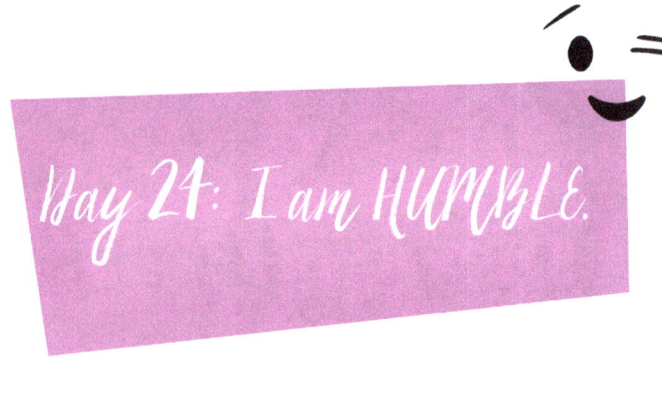

Day 24: I am HUMBLE.

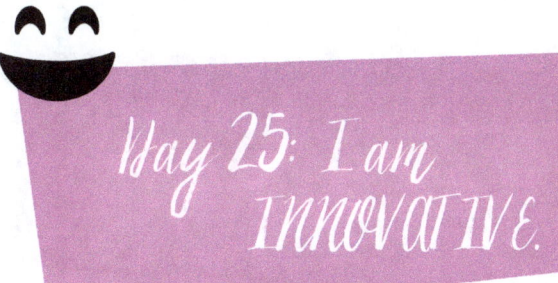

Day 25: I am INNOVATIVE.

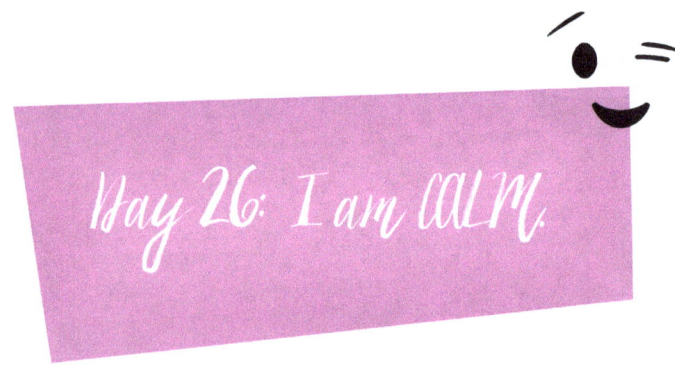

Day 26: I am CALM.

Day 27: I am OPTIMISTIC.

Day 28: I am THANKFUL

Day 29: I am BRAVE.

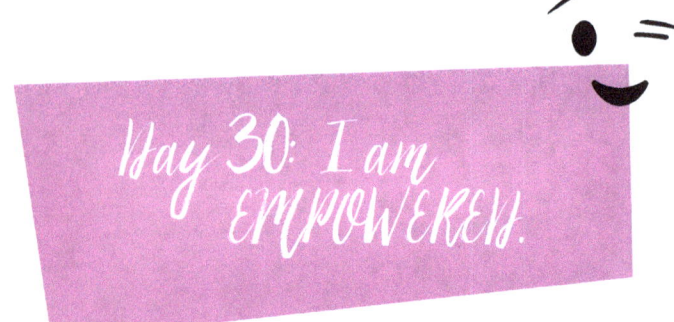

Day 30: I am EMPOWERED.

If you have made it to the end of this journal and completed each of #TheOrieGirls Challenges, you have successfully demonstrated true #GIRLPOWER! It is our hope that you will never forget how special you are. You have written some very important pieces of yourself in the pages of this journal and it will never be forgotten. When we write our feelings, it gives us power. If you remember nothing else that we have shared with you, always remember that all of the power that you will ever need is inside of you.

#THEORIEGIRLS

About the Authors

London B. Orie
THE DAUGHTER | SISTER

London Blake Orie is the youngest member of THE ORIE GIRLS and has her eyes on success. After uttering these words "Mommy, I want to be a writer just like you", London began writing her first book "My Emojis", the debut work of the #GIRLPOWER Series. London has already completed two additional books and can't wait to share them with the world!

In addition to writing, London enjoys acting, singing, dancing and giving back to her community. London plans to embark upon her first book tour following the release of her book in September of 2017.

Follow London Orie's journey at www.TheOrieGirls.com.

About the Authors

Ardre Orie
THE MOTHER

Ardre Orie is a writer, book publisher, playwright, film director and advocate on a mission to create meaningful media that reflects the diversity of our life's experiences and feeds our souls. As the product of a single parent home and childhood survivor of domestic violence, Ardre recognized that there was great power in the transparency of her pain through storytelling. Her goal as a media maven is to create platforms and media that allow the voices of those who have suffered from oppressive circumstances to be heard. Orie has written for a host of clients representing a myriad of networks and brands, including VH1, Bravo, WETV, YouTube and the sports and entertainment industry as well as a bevy of everyday heroes.

In 2015, Orie founded 13th & Joan, a multimedia publishing company to provide a vehicle for aspiring authors, playwrights and film directors to tell their stories with her support and guidance. Orie tirelessly coaches clients onward to success.

Orie continues to thrive as the "Queen of Storytelling" while creating a rich legacy of love. Ardre Orie currently resides in Chicago, Illinois with her husband and two daughters.

Follow Ardre Orie's journey at www.IAMArdreOrie.com.

Connect with The Orie Girls on Social Media

FACEBOOK:
www.facebook.com/theoriegirls

INSTAGRAM:
www.instagram.com/theoriegirls

www.TheOrieGirls.com

WRITE TO #THEORIEGIRLS

13th & Joan
500 N. Michigan Avenue
Chicago, IL 60611

www.ingramcontent.com/pod-product-compliance
Lightning Source LLC
Chambersburg PA
CBHW070622300426
44113CB00010B/1618